8/22

PRI...

Cole...

5

A selection of quotes,
most of which originally appeared
in PRIVATE EYE's
'Colemanballs' column.
Our thanks once again
to the readers who
sent us their
contributions.

If you enjoyed this book,
the best-selling first
Colemanballs
is still available, as are
Colemanballs 2, 3 and 4

COLEMANBALLS TOP TEN

Place	Name	Entries
1	David Coleman	64
2	Murray Walker	48
3	Simon Bates	35
4	Ted Lowe	33
5	Ron Pickering	25
6	Peter Jones	23
7	Harry Carpenter	21
8	Brian Moore	17
9	Byron Butler	15
10	Trevor Bailey	14

Composite total figures compiled by the Neasden Institute of Statistics, E&OE

PRIVATE EYE

Colemanballs

5

Compiled and edited by
BARRY FANTONI

Illustrated by Larry

PRIVATE EYE · CORGI

Published in Great Britain
by Private Eye Publications Ltd
6 Carlisle Street W1V 5RG
in association with Corgi Books

Reprinted 1993

© 1990 Pressdram Ltd
ISBN 0 552 13751 0

Designed by Bridget Tisdall
Printed in Great Britain by
Cox & Wyman Ltd, Reading

Corgi Books are published by Transworld Publishers Ltd,
61-63 Uxbridge Road, Ealing, London W5 5SA,
in Australia by Transworld Publishers (Australia) Pty Ltd,
15–25 Helles Avenue, Moorebank, NSW 2170,
and in New Zealand by Transworld Publishers (NZ) Ltd,
3 William Pickering Drive, Albany, Auckland.

Athletics

"A fairly casual start this, from Bile. He always rushes to the back of the field."

STEVE OVETT

"Behind them there's a whole vanguard of other competitors."

BRENDAN FOSTER

"And as the dancers part they come together with dramatic effect."

DAVID COLEMAN

"Zola Budd is just a pawn in the whole equation."
JOHN BRYANT

"The crowd stood to their feet."
ANITA LONSBOROUGH

"I hope to come first or second, or at least win it."
PETER ELLIOTT

"He's doing well . . . he's letting his legs do the running."
BRENDAN FOSTER

"There's a heart of steel burning inside him."
DAVID MOORCROFT

DAVID COLEMAN: "What made you think it was Richard Gough?"
LIZ McCOLGAN: "Because it looks like him."
"A QUESTION OF SPORT" BBC1

"The wind is absolutely still."
DAVID COLEMAN

". . . and they're limping along very smartly indeed!"
DAVID COLEMAN

"The more experienced runners . . . putting all that training and practice into theory."
JOHN ANDERSON

"And this all-British field means that we will, of course, see a British winner in the men's 400m this evening."
JIM ROSENTHAL

"Not that people had written you off, but they didn't think you'd win anything."
ARCHIE MACPHERSON

"When you're in Korea, you have to eat as the Romans do."

TONY FRANCIS

"They enjoy running on the softer, and in fact harder, course . . ."

DAVID COLEMAN

"But to paraphrase a famous saying, who cares?"

ALAN PARRY

". . . Coe, winding down the curtain on an era of days gone by . . ."

COMMENTATOR RADIO 2

"Running an 800 metre race is a bit like the laws of gravity. If you go too fast it catches up with you eventually."

ADRIAN MOORHOUSE

"If we're talking positively, I can't see no reason why Christie can't get a medal."

JOHN WALKER

"That's thirty-five yards if it's a day . . ."

DESMOND LYNAM

"And Cram's ankle injury is another headache the selectors could do without . . ."

GWR SPORT

Bowls

JIMMY DAVIDSON: "As a journalist, Gordon, you'll find it difficult to find the words to describe this game?"

GORDON DUNWOODIE: "Yes, Jimmy, it's much easier to just sit here and talk about it."

Boxing

"I've got some years on my chest now, and the winds not blowing them off!"

FRANK BRUNO

"The Dutch boxer, Tuur, can speak four languages, which is amazing for someone so short."

NBC COMMENTATOR

"The referee's done very well. He's let the fight flow, as they say in football."

REG GUTTERIDGE

"And there he is sitting in exactly the same place on the other side of the ring."

HARRY CARPENTER

"Mason has won none of his first round fights within the first round, and this isn't one of them . . ."

HARRY CARPENTER

"I'm not going to predict what I'm gonna do, but I'm gonna come out there the winner."

FRANK BRUNO

"Cane, the greatest moment of his boxing life dangling in front of him . . ."

HARRY CARPENTER

"He [Tyson] is strutting around like a leopard."
BBC COMMENTATOR

"On the night, Mitchell's experience carried the day."
JIM McDONNELL

"Chris Blake of Croydon fought Clinton McKenzie at Croydon, but that wasn't home turf because both of them come from Croydon."
REG GUTTERIDGE

"After this fight he [Kirkland Lang] can look himself in the face."

ROD DOUGLAS

"A boxer makes a comeback for one of two reasons: either he's broke or he needs the money."

ALAN MINTER

"I only hope people will come along in peace and enjoy a good fight."

MICKEY DUFF

"I aim to prove that I'm the boxer some people say I am, and some people say I'm not."

GARY MASON

Cricket

"Of his [Botham's] innings yesterday, soon said least mended, I think."

JACK BANNISTER

"Everything was falling around beside him."

TOM GRAVENEY

"On the first day Logie decided to chance his arm and it came off."

TREVOR BAILEY

Q: "Do you feel that the selectors and yourself have been vindicated by this result?"
A: "I don't think the press are vindictive. They can write what they want."

MIKE GATTING

"The lights are shining quite darkly . . ."

HENRY BLOFELD

"You seem to be batting into sticky water."

MIKE SCOTT

"I hope no one's house is burning down. It's much too nice a day to be left without a house."

HENRY BLOFELD

". . . and then South Africa came and took a large slice of the cream."

TONY LEWIS

". . . and Jack Russell was LBW bowled Lawson for a typically dogged 42."

DOMINIC ALLEN

"You always feel that Paul Parker is about to spring into action . . . he is like an uncoiled spring."

CHRISTOPHER MARTIN JENKINS

"That should arrest the non-movement of the score board."

NEVILLE OLIVER

"... You're never too old to stop learning."
IAN BOTHAM

"It is now possible they could get the impossible
score they first thought possible."
CHRISTOPHER MARTIN JENKINS

"I hurt my thumb and then obviously the mother-
in-law died."
MIKE GATTING

"And I suppose, per head of population, a really tremendous ovation from this crowd . . ."

TOM GRAVENEY

"There's Kallicharah chasing after it, his legs going even faster than he is!"

HENRY BLOFELD

"I'll decide when I write my obituary."

IAN BOTHAM

"Unfortunately there have been a few niggles in the woodpile in the last few years."

RAY ILLINGWORTH

"We can all pick our teams, and it wouldn't be a million miles together."

DAVID LLOYD

"It was a great error of misjudgment."

HENRY BLOFELD

"Australia 602 for 6 dec., England 20 for 3. And in the 5th Test, victory is possibly slipping away from England . . ."

STEVE RIDER

"He's doing the best he can do – he's making the worst of a bad job."

FRED TRUMAN

"When you think Roger Harper has a double-hundred on this tour, it makes you realise that he's probably a better batsman than you realise."

IAN BOTHAM

"And the score goes on to 345 for 3. 345 – a certain symmetry there."

HENRY BLOFELD

"That's what batting's all about – knowing where the stumps are."

RAY ILLINGWORTH

"That strike rate, just under forty deliveries a ball."
JACK BANNISTER

Cycling

"He's a favourite for the Tour de France – well an outsider anyway."

PHIL LIGGETT

"He's coming on in fits and bounds."

PHIL LIGGETT

Darts

"The Embassy is the big one. It's the Wimbledon of tennis."

ERIC BRISTOW

Football

"That's the kind he normally knocks in in his sleep – with his eyes closed."

ARCHIE MACPHERSON

"We're back to 1–1."

JOHN MOTSON

"MacMahon is full of appetite."

COMMENTATOR

"Viv Anderson, he's a good jumper – he jumps out of nothing."

RON GREENWOOD

"A rather staccato start in every sense, to the second half."

JOHN MOTSON

"I couldn't but fail to notice the great team spirit in the camp."

TREVOR FRANCIS

"Charlie Redmond's penalty miss will cause him nightmares for many sleepless nights."

MICK DUNNE

"They [Athletic Madrid] are the sort of club who will spend a million pounds without batting an eyeball."

RON ATKINSON

"We've got to sit down and have a think about where we stand."

ROY McFARLAND

"Chapman floundering in the mud like some huge white elephant . . ."

CAPITAL RADIO

"Sheedy balances up the midfield with that magic wand of a left foot."

JIMMY HILL

"There was a lovely bit of play which set Valley Parade alight again."

JIMMY ARMFIELD

"Ian St John there, sitting on the fence again – but I must say, this time I agree with him . . ."

ALAN PARRY

"Hearts 2 Motherwell 0. A good fight back there by Motherwell who were 2 – 0 down at one stage."

PADDY FEENY

"He had several better options than shooting himself there."

RON ATKINSON

"I think the Italians have got their hands cut out tonight."

TREVOR FRANCIS

"Houghton got up like a tree blown down in a storm."

PETER JONES

"Seventeen minutes gone and already no goals . . ."

RON JONES

"Great save there by Snelders. The Dutchman there, stemming the dyke."

ARCHIE MACPHERSON

"And who can forget that memorable match last time between these sides, when I think the score was four–three . . ."

DEREK JOHNSTONE

"Celtic will be glad to be sitting in the bath now with two points tucked under their belt."

JOHN GREIG

"That really seemed the Gobi desert there – not a red shirt anywhere."

BILL McLAREN

"In a European tie both legs are equally important, if not more important than each other."

COLIN CALDER

"Gascoigne, booed every time he has touched the ball, has remained totally anonymous."

PETER JONES

"It was a goal of really simple simplicity . . ."

LBC

"These lads from Everton are making a one in a million trip to Wembley, for the second time in four years."

TONY GUBBA

"Sadly, the immortal Jackie Milburn died recently."

CLIFF MORGAN

"It's definitely the quickest football I've played in. What we try and do is slow it down and play a slower kind of football."

RAY WILKINS

"Albion face their stiffest task yet in the freezing hothouse at Sunderland."

MALCOLM BOYDEN

"Any two teams can win this match."

JOHN GREIG

"My legs sort of disappeared from nowhere."

CHRIS WADDLE

"We're flying on Concorde. That'll shorten the distance. That's self-explanatory."

BOBBY ROBSON

"We could have taken the lead before we even scored."

PETER BEARDSLEY

"Well, I think Arsenal will either win or lose the championship this year."

GRAHAM TAYLOR

"At the end of the day, it's nil–nil at half time."

RAY CLEMENCE

"It's all in the melting point now."

BOBBY ROBSON

"It's been a first half in keeping with the whole of the match."

MARTIN TYLER

"Brian Clough wields a tight ship."

GABRIEL CLARK

"Southall's goal kick breaks off Venison's head."

CLIVE TYLDESLEY

"We didn't expect to be top, and that's a fact. But football's not about facts, it's about what happens."

DAVE BASSETT

"Many supporters say they wouldn't stand for all-seater stadiums."

GUY MICHELMORE

"You know, the Brazilians aren't as good as they used to be, or as they are now."

KENNY DALGLEISH

"Omens are there to be broken."

BOB WILSON

"Rush was there quick as a needle."

PETER JONES

"And with 35 minutes gone, it's Barcelona 2, Sofia 1. Just the kind of result we were expecting at this stage, except that the Bulgarians have scored."

JOHN HELM

"He accepted the benefit of the flag."

RON ATKINSON

"Stuart Pearce, who leads from the front, even though he plays at the back."

DAVID PLEAT

"The rest of your football team are very tall . . . they dwarf above you."

FRED DINEAGE

"Some of the fans come on the pitch and shake the players on the back of the chest!"

MIKE MORRIS

". . . 18 months ago they [Sweden] were arguably one of the three best teams in Europe, and that would include Germany and Holland and Russia and . . . anybody else if you like."

BOBBY ROBSON

"The game finely balanced with Celtic well on top . . ."

JOHN GREIG

"The score is Liverpool 0, Norwich 0, and it's only the absence of a goal that we're waiting for."

COMMENTATOR

"Norman's greatest quality has always been his quality."

RON ATKINSON

"There's never been a good time to score an own goal against yourself."

JOHN GREIG

". . . home advantage gives you an advantage . . ."

BOBBY ROBSON

JOHN MOTSON: "Well, Trevor, what does this
substitution mean tactically?"
TREVOR BROOKING: "Well, Barnes has come off
and Roecastle has come on . . ."

BBC TV

"The Roker roar has been very much to the fore in
the background."

COMMENTATOR

"He went down like a sack of potatoes, then made
a meal of it."

TREVOR BROOKING

"If the second half is anything like the first, England will certainly be defending the goal to our right."

COMMENTATOR

"I'm a forgotten man in his [Bobby Robson's] mind."

GLEN HODDLE

"As long as the ball stays out of play, it's just eating into Manchester United's hands."

MIKE INGHAM

"And now for the goals from Carrow Road, where the game ended nil–nil."

ELTON WELSBY

"Here, Liverpool are trying to manfully go forward without a man."

RADIO 2 COMMENTATOR

"I wouldn't pay a million pounds to be somewhere else tonight!"

CAPITAL GOLD COMMENTATOR

"The proof of the pudding is in the eating and Villa aren't pulling up any trees."

TONY BUTLER

"We're very pleased about the way we played because we know we can play like that."

LEROY ROSENIOR

"Well, it's been two ends of the same coin . . ."

DAVE BASSETT

"Elsewhere the big guns were firing on all cylinders."

TONY ADAMSON

"Robson's lack of inspiration has been the cornerstone of United's weakness."

BRIAN MOORE

"The Boss says that games in hand are no good unless you turn them into points. What he's getting at is that games in hand aren't much good unless you turn them into points."

DAVID PLATT

"For a while it looked like George Graham was in danger of being bitten by the hand that used to feed him . . ."

COMMENTATOR

"Fair enough, he was in an offside position, but I don't think he was offside."

JIMMY GREAVES

"We could easily go out and spend £40,000 on a player, but that, of course, is impossible."

BRIAN LITTLE

"If he gets a yard ahead of himself, they won't catch him."

BOBBY ROBSON

"A silence that's been graced by silence at Old Trafford this afternoon . . ."

BRIAN MOORE

"Winning or losing is not the end result."

RADIO 2 COMMENTATOR

"Silas is controlling the midfield for Brazil . . . he's the hubbub of the team."

BOBBY ROBSON

"You don't get any bigger than the quarter-finals of the FA Cup."

ALEX FERGUSON

"This top of the table clash between Chelsea in second place and Manchester United in ninth . . ."

ALAN GREEN

"The chances of Hibernian now qualifying for Europe are hanging by a knife edge."

RADIO BROADLAND

". . . and Davie Cooper, I'm told, has equalised for Motherwell, so it's St Mirren 2, Motherwell 1."

GERRY McNEE

"With the benefit of hindsight are we going to get goals in the second half?"

ELTON WELSBY

"He [Beardsley] is so aware of where his colleagues are. He tried to pick out McMahon, it fell to Houghton."

TONY GUBBA

Golf

"He's got to go in for a hernia operation, but when he gets over that he'll be back in harness again."

PETER ALLIS

"In technical terms, he's making a real pig's ear of this hole."

PETER ALLIS

"Look at that! Right smack in the edge of the rough!"

PETER ALLIS

"If you can imagine a clock face, the wind is coming from about half-past two."

PETER ALLIS

"So he goes from 3 under to 3 over, all in one foul sweep."

RENTON LAIDLAW

Horses

"He's retiring at the height of his pinnacle."
HARVEY SMITH

"He must have discovered euthanasia – he never seems to get any older!"
JOHN FRANCOME

"Not unlike it, but not very like it either."
JOHN OAKSEY

"There you can see Sunday Silence, who's hidden by another horse . . ."
BROUGH SCOTT

"Warrshan, the 3.75 million dollar horse, proved itself to be a million dollars."
JULIAN WILSON

"And he took to it like water to a duck."
RICHARD PITMAN

Literally

"... an Achilles' heel for the Maclaren team this year, and it literally is the heel because it's the gearbox ..."

MURRAY WALKER

"As you all know, the televising of Parliament began almost literally today – in fact, yesterday."

JOHN DUNNE

"When those stalls open, the horses are literally going to explode."

BROUGH SCOTT

"They were literally tied together from start to finish with a string almost."

STEVE OVETT

"This game is literally being played at 100 miles per hour."

DEREK RAE

"And Greig Lemond has literally come back from the dead to lead the Tour de France."

PHIL LIGGETT

"And the 'Pride of Kent' is now literally coming through the Dover harbour wall."

LAURIE MARGOLIS

"There were literally thousands of people in queues, as far as the eye could stretch."

DEREK JAMESON

"Luton scored in the first five minutes while Norwich were still, quite literally, finding their feet."

GERALD SINSTAD

"... with Robert Millar and Gianetti quite literally exploding into the streets of Cardiff."

RICHARD KEAYS

"Klaus, the son of a man who buys and sells and breeds horses. So he was literally born in the saddle."

DEREK THOMPSON

"This horse literally breaks itself in two to clear this wall."

STEPHEN HADLEY

"Australia, with two new caps, literally took France to the cleaners."

COMMENTATOR

Motor Sport

"He [Senna] is almost very definitely in a class of his own with Prost."

MURRAY WALKER

"With modern technology and the fantastic car-to-pits radio, Piquet now knows he can see Prost in front of him."

MURRAY WALKER

"27 points to 12 . . . and the Australians have
eased their cushion a bit further away."

BILL McLAREN

"The motor race was riddled with highlights."

AUSTRALIAN BROADCASTING CORPORATION

"The answer's an affirmative 'Yes'."

NIGEL MANSELL

"Just look at the power of that turbo – he just
walks past him."

JAMES HUNT

"That was exactly the same place where Senna overtook Nannini that he did **not** overtake Alain Prost."

MURRAY WALKER

"Senna now on lap 6 of 65 – just under half distance."

MURRAY WALKER

". . . and I wouldn't like to be sitting in Alain Prost's shoes right now."

BARRY SHEEN

Oddballs

"That's the gravy on the cake."

BARBARA POTTER

"I wish I'd had the hot-dog concession – they'd have sold like hot cakes."

WALLY WHYTON

"But by that stage the death knell had been signed."

RAYMOND SNODDY

"They're hanging on to their hats for grim life."

EVE POLLARD

"If you need something to take your mind off breast feeding, the place to be was Bristol."
JENNY MURRAY

"Police believe that the killers of a man whose burnt and charred body was found in Epping Forest last week may have had a grudge against him."

ROBIN HOUSTON

"Back pain is a headache for doctors and other medical staff."

RADIO PICCADILLY

"Once the milk has been spilt, in this sort of case it's very difficult to put Humpty Dumpty back on the wall again."

PETER CLOWES'S SOLICITOR

"That's nature . . . it's the dog-eat-dog world that these fish live in."

JOHN WILSON

"How fatal is it?"

MIKE MORRIS

"London isn't the largest city, but it's definitely larger than the next largest."

BRIAN HAYES

"I suppose if you let this genie out of the bottle you'd get, to continue the allusion, a whole lot of butterflies out of Pandora's Box . . ."

PRU GOWARD

"The canvas for Radio 4 is as long as a piece of string."

DAVID HATCH

"The wind was coming in like a bacon slicer."

ANN LESLIE

"And now – Russell Grant is bringing us the future before it happens."

MIKE MORRIS

"Incidentally, by the way."

DAVID COLEMAN

"Of course, the Russians aren't used to man-made materials, they're used to synthetics, aren't they?"

VIV LUMSDEN

"Women are more prone to pre-menstrual tension."

DR J. McCORMACK

"It's dog eat dog in this rat race. . ."

JOHN DEACON

"When he's in form he's brilliant. But when he's not, he's not . . ."

MONICA PHELPS

"He's come on in fits and bounds."

PAUL SHERWEN

"I have to say I was riveted to the seat. It really pinned me to the wall all the way through."

JERRY PALMER

"The winds of change are tasting good at the moment."

ANN DIAMOND

"It opens up a whole can of beans for me."

MICHAEL YORK

"And there's fog on the M25 in both directions."

JOHN HUMPHRIES

"We need 633 kilos [of stamps] – I've no idea how heavy that is!"

SIMON MAYO

"We can't sit here and stand for it."

PETER TEMPLE MORRIS

"They seem to be improving, I can't say getting better."

RADIO 4

". . . and Mr Knapp is on the line . . ."

SUE MACGREGOR

"I used to sit in your seat, so I know exactly where you stand."

THE NEW PROFESSIONALS

"The world is so big and so global now."

PAT KANE

"That's a fish of a different feather."

DEREK JAMESON

"Let me then switch tacks and change horses in midstream."

CHRIS DUNKLEY

"Cheer up. It's a sunny day, and we're talking about breast cancer."

PRESENTER, GREATER LONDON RADIO

"You have a real feel for the history of the past, don't you?"

DEREK JAMESON

". . . you'll be able to read it in black and white tomorrow, and if you get the *Financial Times*, you'll see it in pink and white."

DOMINIC HARROD

"You're a sort of Rupert Murdoch of Australia, aren't you?"

EMMA FREUD

"As long as he [Lord Olivier] was alive, he was there."

ALAN BATES

"... and Janet Reger talks about the ups and downs of the ladies underwear business ..."

TRAILER FOR WOMAN'S HOUR

"If you're walking down the street and you don't want to get hit by a meteorite then don't eat eggs."

POULTRY FARMER

"In Africa, 2 out of 3 elephants have been decimated."

DEREK JAMESON

"There is a two mile tail-back at the Dartford Tunnel. This is mainly due to the number of vehicles in the area."

FIONA FARRELL

"A momentary moment of slackness ..."

BBC RADIO SOLENT

"It's another notch in the rung on the slippery slope towards anarchy."

GEORGE GAVIN

"Yes, the Great Fire of London. It started in a baker's shop in Pudding Lane in 1666. I wonder if it's still there?"

DAVE LEE TRAVIS

"In this country we take a paternalistic view of television – hence the great 'Auntie BBC' . . ."

MICHAEL GRADE

"He [Otto Preminger] had his wrist on the pulse of the world."

VINCENT PRICE

"Some of the locals in Swindon have called it the Flying Zebra, mainly because of the blue and yellow stripes on the side of the vehicle."

TRAFFIC POLICEMAN

"After banging your head against a brick wall for long enough you'd think that some of it would rub off."

ALEX MURPHY

"Now here's some Swedish music seen through German ears."

RADIO 3

"He's the one rotten apple who turns out to be the good egg."

WILLIAM FEAVER

"A touch of Vivaldi here – Albinoni's Concerto in D Major."

DEREK JAMESON

". . . he's a fully-fledged internationalist in the making."

FORBES McFALL

". . . they're players who are half a yard quicker in their minds, so their feet don't need to be there."

JIM DUFFY

"It was in this hall last week that an Indian weight-lifter picked up three medals."

IAN PAYNE

"It was a catch 50/50 situation really."

DEAN WILLEY

"You say you've hit some dodgy ground. Exactly what does that mean in layman's terms."

GUY MICHELMORE

"The Spirella corset factory is closing because the bottom has dropped out of the market."

ANGLIA TV

"The problem is that there are so many people alive in the Soviet Union now who gave their lives for that sort of thing."

JAMES DINGLEY

"The hurdles we had to climb were traditionally untrodden . . . so we were blazing new trails all the time."

POWER EXPERT

"Where do lions come in the pecking order?"
SARAH KENNEDY

"[Engineering work] . . .should not interfere with
your viewing of ITV programmes, however there
will be times when we are off the air completely."
ITV ANNOUNCEMENT

"It's a terrible thing when you can't walk the streets even in your own home."

MARGARET WILKINS

"The reality could not be further from the truth."

BBC PRESENTER

"Paul, I don't know what your hobbies are, so the book I'm sending you is *Surviving The Killing Fields*."

JULIE WEBSTER

"Who knows – they may be one step up that gang-plank on the plane to Australia."

HENRY KELLY

"Orange juice; that's the juice of an orange."

MICHAEL BARRY

"If I can't understand it , what chance has the general public got?"

DEREK JAMESON

"Appearing at the event will be the late son of Tommy Cooper."

SIMON WHITE

"People with HIV infection can remain healthy for a long time, sometimes many years, perhaps for the rest of their natural lives, perhaps forever."

RADIO 4

"Fame? It's a double-edged coin really."

VICTOR KIAM

"I can hear the BBC clock ticking silently away."

PETER DICKSON

"On BBC2 shortly Clive James and his guests will be discussing Christianity and its relevance to Christmas."

CONTINUITY ANNOUNCER

"They were standing there like sitting ducks."

RICHARD THOMPSON

"The remaining guests have virtually left."

DAVID DIMBLEBY

"We should be barking up the wrong tree to go down that road!"

PROFESSOR PATRICK MYNDFOOT

". . . diet is one jigsaw in the whole map."

EVERTON F C DIETICIAN

"The Screen Actors Guild has 72,000 members. Out of those thousands, a handful are relegated to that rarefied atmosphere known as stardom . . ."
MICHELLE LEE

"He should put his foot down with a firm hand."
RADIO BROADLAND

"Do they have to dig holes in the actual water?"
DEREK JAMESON

"There've been moments of excitement and not inconsiderate skill."
GEORGE BAILEY

"As the caterpillar approaches the larva stage it becomes more sluggish."

CHANNEL 4

"The Portuguese, being a sea-faring nation, are always happy at the side of a lake."

TERRY WOGAN

"Now, we all know about hash-browns, what are they?"

JUDY FINNIGAN

"We're at the gates, ready to take the city by storm – verbally speaking, of course."

DEREK JAMESON

"Michael Bentine, you're a Peruvian by birth but born and raised in England."

ROBIN RAY

"This parade marks the bicentenary of the storming of the Bastille some time ago. Two hundred years ago, in fact."

JEREMY PAXMAN

"Renton, you're a great traveller. Every day of the
year you're somewhere in the world!"

GARY RICHARDSON

"Condoms are not usually subjected to rigorous
tests. As trading standards officers, we are
responsible for controls on every conceivable
product on the market."

HAMPSHIRE TRADING STANDARDS OFFICER

Politics

"Businessmen should stand or fall on their own two feet."

EDWINA CURRIE

"You have only to fly over it or go in a helicopter."

NICHOLAS RIDLEY

INTERVIEWER: "Why did you decide to put your head above the parapet on this issue?"
TODAY: "To gauge the temperature of the water."

TODAY

"Kinnock's not prepared to put his button on the trigger."

ELEANOR GOODMAN

"Our members will be grasping the bull by the horns only to find that it's a damp squib."

A TRADE UNION LEADER

"I believe that all illegal organisations should be outlawed."

REV IAN PAISLEY

"Ireland's been put on the political back-burner and no one wants to grasp that nettle."

MICHAEL YARDLEY

"What we have is a person who was publicly discredited in public . . ."

PADDY ASHDOWN

"Yes, in the end all tunnels make money, the Severn Bridge, the Dartford Tunnel . . ."

TONY RICHARDS

"It is a hothouse in a goldfish bowl."

NEIL KINNOCK

"The Prime Minister pulled a bomb-shell on them."

JOHN COLE

"I think I can scotch that one on the head straight away."

SIR JEREMY THOMAS

"Would you say the writing's on the wall for Le Pen?"

PETER DEELEY

"I really expected it to go one way or the other tonight."

JOHN MACKAY

"Mrs Thatcher's silence has resounded like thunder across Britain."

PADDY ASHDOWN

"I call on Fred Jarvis to ask his members to stand ready to sit down. That would be a giant step forward."

CALL NICK ROSS

"This is the advent of a new beginning of continued change."

RONALD REAGAN

"There's one thing that the troubles in Belfast won't kill – and that's the people."

GEORGE BEST

". . . that Nigel Lawson has been able to pull off a hat trick for two budgets running."

COLIN W. McLEAN

"Thanks Tony, and how long will this 24 hour rail strike last?"

EAMONN O'NEAL

"The new Margam Colliery has yet to get off the ground."

ARTHUR SCARGILL

"The Government has really put the clay among the pigeons."

BRIAN REDHEAD

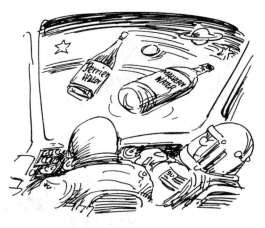

"There's a lot of uncharted waters in space."
DAN QUAYLE

"There's no smoke without mud being flung
around."

EDWINA CURRIE

"The two super-powers cannot divide the world
into their oyster."

MICHAEL HESELTINE

"Neutrality doesn't make sense – who are they
neutral against?"

DENIS HEALEY

"The road to communism appears plain sailing."

IAN GLOVER-JAMES

"British Rail stabbed us in the back by blowing the talks out of the water before they even got off the ground."

JIMMY KNAPP

"Always remember, the Russians are fantastic chess players, and I suspect Mr Gorbachev has still quite a few cards left in his hand."

JACQUES DARRAS

"Does that mean it could be a damp squib that might blow up in the face of the Government?"

RADIO 4 NEWSCASTER

"To break the two party monopoly will be very difficult."

DAVID OWEN

"Isn't that stretching belief beyond all possible credulity?"

NEIL KINNOCK

Pop

"The chickens haven't come home to roost yet, so the band's still playing."

ROGER ALTMAN

"It's not original in the sense of originality."

EDWIN STARR

". . . regardless of all that, taking all that into account . . ."

MIKE BATT

"That wasn't the 1964 version but, for a change, the 1972 version. Because on this show we like to look forward as well as back."

STEVE JONES

"That illness cemented the relationship in every sense of the word."

SIMON BATES

"Let's stay with the colour green because the next track is called 'New Shade of Blue'."

BOB POWEL

"I'd like to play Scrooge in *Oliver Twist*."

LUKE FROM BROS

"Bangkok is probably the most unique city in the world."

SIMON BATES

"He lived between 1500 and 1559 and this is true
– he was a real descendant of mine."

SIMON MAYO

"Just one of those songs that sticks in your ear
like quicksilver . . ."

SIMON BATES

"What's your name, Kate?"

SIMON BATES

"If ever I'm going to write an autobiography I'll get my ex-minder to write it, because he's got such a good imagination."

SHEENA EASTON

"Thanks to everyone at that club – in Harlow, I think it was – for making it such a memorable night."

STEVE WRIGHT

"It was a whole new can of beans in every sense of the word."

SIMON BATES

"Frank Loesser . . . one of the unsung heroes of popular music."

DAVID JACOBS

"Of course, Bros have always been popular; it's just taken people a long time to realise it."

ADRIAN JOHN

"It's a coincidence all by itself . . ."

SIMON BATES

"He comes at you rather like a fridge door opening with the light going on."

SIMON BATES

"I mean, what are juke boxes now? 20 pence maximum, 10 pence at most."

STEVE WRIGHT

"Either he [Roy Orbison] kept it all inside, or he was a stoic."

PAUL GAMBACCINI

"The image of a blackman with a ghettoblaster on his shoulder is just a stereotype!"

YVONNE BREWSTER

"Dr Hook, well in the forefront of the top 3, at number 3."

ALAN FREEMAN

"I'm not sure how many questions we've actually answered today – we've probably posed as many as we've set."

BOB HALL

Royalty

"The grouse are in absolutely no danger from people who shoot grouse."

HRH PRINCE PHILIP

Rugby

"We're making chances, Derek, and as long as you make chances you've a chance."

JOHN GREIG

"The most dramatic rugby – you couldn't have written it in *Roy of the Rovers*."

NIGEL STARMER-SMITH

"I said before the game that it might take all season for Armstrong and Chalmers to become an overnight success. I was wrong, they did it overnight!"

IAN ROBERTSON

"Now the All Blacks thunderbolt is moving slowly forward . . ."

IAN ROBERTSON

"I wouldn't be at all surprised if there's a shock result this afternoon."

JOHN GREIG

"The Rosslyn Park captain now on the other side
of the receiving end of the table, so to speak."

NIGEL STARMER-SMITH

"Skill is the name of the game and Widnes have it in gay abundance."

DAVID WATKINS

"Being seven points behind gives you a definite psychological advantage."

ALEX MURPHY

"That was perfection of the highest quality."

ALEX MURPHY

Snooker

"That's the sportsmanship you find in snooker,
Terry asked Jimmy for a rub of his sandpaper."
JOHN VIRGO

"It seems that Cliff Wilson's found his potting
boots."
TED LOWE

"There's the referee . . . any rowdy people and he puts on his Sergeant Major voice and they are eliminated."

TED LOWE

"At his best, Mountjoy wasn't as good as he is now."

TED LOWE

"Although a Canadian, Mario Martinez is, in fact, an Italian."

TED LOWE

"Going through Jimmy White's mind now will be the winning post."

DENNIS TAYLOR

"Whoever wins the first frame will be one frame up."

STEVE DAVIS

"He came from 5 – 0 down to beat John Virgo 5 – 2."

JOHN SPICER

"The man in the driving seat is now at the table."
TED LOWE

"I don't know what shot Cliff played there, but
I'm sure it wasn't the shot he has played."
JOHN SPENCER

Superbowl

"Although he isn't as good as he was two years
ago, now he's even better!"
COMMENTATOR

Tennis

"For those of you who believe in these things, it's taken him 13 points to break the serve, it's the 13th of the month today, this is the 13th Benson & Hedges Championship . . . and yesterday was his 24th birthday."

JOHN BARRETT

"But now he has to consummate the lead . . . and that's not always easy."

MARK COX

"Steffi Graf has now won 42 consecutive matches, winning all of them."

CHRISTINE JANES

"He seems to have found a chink in Chang's armour."

DAVID MERCER

"He certainly looks older than he did last year."

MARK COX

"He's wise enough in the ways of the world to realise he's got to play as many balls as he can."

GERALD WILLIAMS

"The question marks must float through your mind like bees in a storm."

FREW McMILLAN

"As for Lendl. . . his thorn in the crown is a shoulder injury."

PAM DIXON

"Cahill's courage . . . courage one can expect from a man whose father captains an Adelaide bowls team."

BBC COMMENTATOR

"Michael Chang is very young but mature in years."

PAUL HUTCHINGS

"The fact that he has won has probably done him more good than harm."

FREW McMILLAN

"That was an absolutely booming second service, it took off like a parachute."

GERALD WILLIAMS

"Steffi [Graf] has a tremendous presence when you're standing right next to her."

VIRGINIA WADE

"The rain must be frustrating for those driving along a motorway who desperately want to see some tennis."

FREW McMILLAN